# DEADLY SCIENCE

## Life cycles

**Contents:**

ADJUNCT ASSOCIATE PROFESSOR COREY TUTT OAM

## DEADLYSCIENCE

DeadlyScience aims to provide Science, Technology, Engineering and Mathematics (STEM) resources to remote schools around Australia. So far, DeadlyScience has shipped more than shipped more than 33,000 STEM books and resources to more than 800 schools across the country.

The organisation began when proud Kamilaroi man Corey Tutt found out that some schools in Australia were completely under-resourced and that Aboriginal and Torres Strait Islander children were discouraged from pursuing STEM because of this. DeadlyScience knows from personal experience that books and resources change lives and believes these kids deserve nothing but the best. Aboriginal and Torres Strait Islander peoples in Australia were the First Scientists of this land, and DeadlyScience is committed to preserving that history.

# Living things

All living creatures have life cycles. Animals and plants are born or germinated, mature, reproduce and live in ways that are determined not only by their biology but also by their environment and the other creatures they live with. There can be huge variations in life cycles too, such as with the immortal jellyfish, which can revert to a juvenile stage if it experiences environmental or physical stress. Animals can be classified as vertebrates or invertebrates based on whether or not they have a spine.

**RED KANGAROO**

A red kangaroo is bawurra in the Gamilaraay language.

## Birds

Australia has more than 930 bird species, including more parrot species than any place on Earth. Birds have a body covering of feathers and special anatomy that gives them the power of flight, except for ratites like the southern cassowary and some ground-dwelling or marine species. All birds lay eggs and have beaks or bills. They also lack teeth, although some chicks have a sharp 'egg tooth' they use to crack open the eggshell from the inside on hatching.

In the Dharug language, the word for bird is binyang.

## Reptiles

Reptiles – such as turtles, lizards, snakes and crocodiles – mostly cannot easily thermoregulate (or control their own body temperature internally). Most lay eggs, although some lizards and snakes birth live young. Their skin is usually thin and watertight, protected by scales or scutes. Reptiles shed their skin as they grow, which means young reptiles shed more than old ones. They tend to be well camouflaged and solitary.

## Mammals

With the exception of the egg-laying monotremes (the platypus and echidna), mammals give birth to live young they feed with milk. Most are warm-blooded and have fur or hair. The group includes such diverse animals as humans, dogs, cats, whales, bats, monkeys and seals. Some, known as marsupials, give birth to very underdeveloped young that continue to grow in the mother's pouch after birth. Some species live together in groups or families, but others live solitary lives.

Blue-tongued lizard is thalagal in the Gamilaraay language.

FACT
There are about 1000 wattle species in Australia, including wuanga in the Noongar language, and nanggil in Bundjalung.

**CLOWNFISH**
The word for fish is magura in Dharug.

**GREEN TREE FROG**
The word frog in the Noongar language is kweeyar.

## Plants

Although the term 'plant' is broad, we generally think of land plants when we use it. Land plants obtain energy through photosynthesis, creating food from light, water and carbon dioxide. Plants have close ecological relationships with animals, relying on them to pollinate and disperse their seeds; in turn, plants supply animals with shelter and food. Some plants only live for one year before dying, while others live for many years.

## Amphibians

Frogs, salamanders, newts and toads are amphibians, and they're all cold-blooded. Amphibians need to stay moist, and they often live in or near water. They tend to have muscular tongues that can be extended. Most amphibians lay eggs in the water, which hatch larvae that undergo a process of metamorphosis into adult forms. Frogs and toads use calls and noises to send messages, attract their mate, and to emit warnings.

**DID YOU KNOW?**

**Invertebrates are animals that don't have a backbone. These animals include insects, molluscs, corals, crustaceans, arachnids, jellyfish and worms. This is a diverse grouping with varied characteristics.**

Scorpion is thula in the Gamilaraay language.

## Fish

Fish are mostly cold-blooded animals that live in water, breathing through gills. They are covered in scales or scaly skin and have fins. Most fish species have highly developed senses, such as sight, taste and smell. Many can also detect motion and vibration through specialised receptors and glands.

## Totems

Across Australia, plant and animal totems are inherited by families as their spiritual emblem. They provide guidance for people's roles and responsibilities within their communities, Creation and Country. Totems are decided by an Elder and are given during a Coming of Age Ceremony. The Wadawurrung people of the Kulin Nation use the black crow as one of their totems. It symbolises wisdom and strength.

Black crow is waagaan in the Gamilaraay language.

# Sunflowers

These tall, bright, summer-growing plants are native to North America, but they are grown commercially and domestically in Queensland and New South Wales. Their seeds are pressed to produce oil that's used for cooking, as well as in paints, cosmetics and lubricants, and as fuel. Sunflower seeds are also delicious to eat.

## GROWTH ESSENTIALS

### Sunlight

The sun is our source of energy, heat and light. Plants need sunlight to perform photosynthesis. Some animals rely on the sun for heat, and even nocturnal animals feed on living things that get their energy from the sun.

### Water

All living things need water. Plants need water for photosynthesis, and animals rely on it for hydration and digestion – some even live in it!

### Air

The atmosphere that surrounds our world is a mixture of oxygen, carbon dioxide and nitrogen. Plants take in carbon dioxide for photosynthesis and expel oxygen. In contrast, animals breathe in oxygen from the air or water and breathe out carbon dioxide.

### Nutrients

Organisms need nutrients to function properly, to stay healthy, and to grow. Plants make their own sugars and absorb nutrients in the soil through their roots. Animals eat other animals or plants to get nutrients.

### Shelter

Every organism needs somewhere to live. They need safe, regular access to their other growth essentials, as well as protection from the weather.

Nutrient-packed sunflower seeds.

**STAGE 1**

Sunflower seeds are just 10–15 mm long and 4 mm wide, and grow inside a hard hull. There are about 1000 in the centre of a flower; each contains the beginnings of a new plant, as well as food for the plant as it grows. When it is buried in soil and watered, it starts to evolve. This is the beginning of germination.

Mitika means flower in the language of the Kaurna people of South Australia.

**STAGE 4**

The flower blooms. In the centre of the flower are the parts needed to make more seeds: stamens and carpels. Insects such as bees feed on the flower's nectar, and when they sit on the plant, they pick up pollen from the stamens. When they switch flowers, they deposit this pollen. This fertilises the carpels of the next flower, which allows eggs inside the flower head to become new seeds. The petals will fall off while the plant grows new seeds, which will be collected by farmers, dropped onto the ground or spread by animals such as birds and mice.

## STAGE 2

The seed's outer shell will split open, and a root will grow downwards into the soil. A shoot will then grow outwards from the soil to the surface. Eventually, the outer shell of the seed falls off, and small leaves open up. This tiny shoot is called a seedling. Over time it grows taller, thicker and stronger.

**MONARCH BUTTERFLY**

Butterfly is balabalaa in the Gamilaraay language.

**DID YOU KNOW?**

**Each sunflower head produces 1000–2000 sunflower seeds!**

## STAGE 3

Now that the plant has leaves, it can make its own food by using sunlight to process air, and water to create energy. This process is called photosynthesis. The leaves need to collect as much sun as possible, as well as carbon dioxide, through tiny holes on the surface. The plant also soaks up water and nutrients through its roots from the soil. This is the point in its life when it will grow the fastest. Shortly, a green flower bud will form.

A green flower bud grows next.

# Banksias

Banksias grow as trees or woody shrubs. Australia has lots of different types of banksia, but they all have similar flowers that stand upright on one spike. They are usually yellow, but sometimes they have orange, red, pink and even violet flowers.

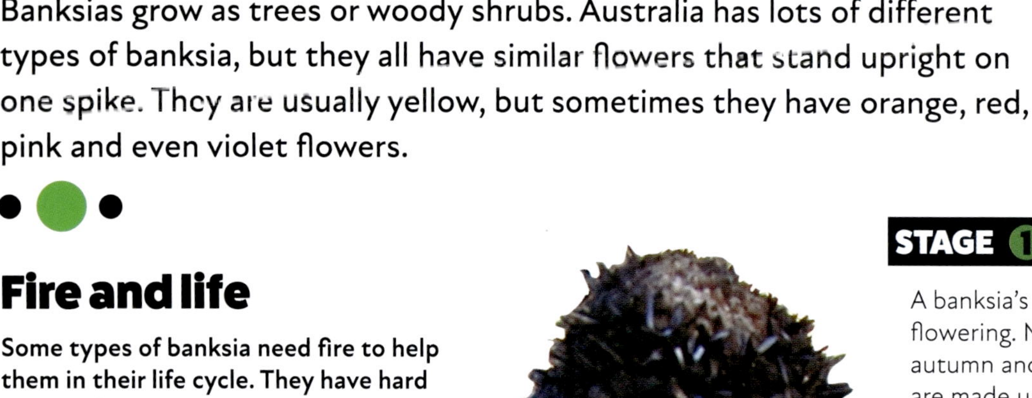

## Fire and life

**Some types of banksia need fire to help them in their life cycle. They have hard seed pods that will only open if they are dried out completely or heated by fire. Fire has been a vital force in the Australian landscape for millions of years. As a result, a large proportion of the continent's plants are dependent on fire to complete their life cycles – many seeds won't be released and some won't be germinated unless stimulated by the heat or smoke of a bushfire. This includes banksias, hakeas, sheoaks, grevilleas and native pines.**

**However, too-frequent fires are as much of a problem as too few. After each blaze, even fire-loving plants, such as banksias, need time for their seeds to germinate and mature into adult trees, before they can produce flowers and seeds in time for the next inferno to sweep through their area.**

Birds, bees and other insects pollinate banksias.

**STAGE 1**

A banksia's life cycle begins with the tree flowering. Many banksias flower over autumn and winter. The flower heads are made up of hundreds (sometimes thousands) of tiny individual flowers grouped together in pairs. Flowers are then pollinated by birds and insects.

**STAGE 4**

Once the seeds find their way back to the soil, they begin to grow into seedlings. The banksia will then continue to grow until it reaches adulthood at about two years old. Then the life cycle starts all over again.

**FACT**

Australia has more than 170 types of banksia, and some grow to 30 m tall.

Banksia is wurindaga in the Gumbaynggirr language.

## STAGE 2

After the plants have flowered and are pollinated, they produce fruits. The fruits of banksias are called follicles, and they are hard, woody and often grouped together in a similar way to pine cones. The fruits protect the seeds from animals and from being too wet or drying out too early.

## STAGE 3

During late spring and early summer, the fruits dry out and the seed pods begin to open. The seeds are then eaten by birds or fall to the ground. Some seeds are very light and are carried away on the breeze. The birds fly to new places, and the seeds work their way through the bird and are then pooped out, ready to germinate and grow.

### DID YOU KNOW?

**Some First Nations communities use banksia cones to strain their water; others soak the flowers to create a sweet drink from the nectar.**

# Bees

Bees are flying insects that produce honey and pollinate much of our food supply. You may have seen bees buzzing around flowers. If you watch closely, you'll see them crawl right down into a flower – they are collecting nectar.

A bee will carry a load of nectar from a lot of flowers back to the hive. Bees then use their wings to move air in order to evaporate most of the water. What's left is honey. Baby bees eat honey to help them grow.

## Best buds

Plants spread their pollen via pollinators such as bees and birds, or through environmental elements, such as wind or water. Plants reproduce by self-pollination or cross-pollination, which is when fertilisation occurs between different plants of the same species.

Pollinators are attracted by the promise of food in the form of pollen or nectar. Many flowers use bright colours and scents to entice pollinators. Some have evolved to mimic naturally occurring pheromones, such as the hammer orchid, which omits the odour of a female wasp, luring male wasps. Some pollinators have developed special relationships with particular flowers; for example, brush-tipped tongues or elongated noses provide a great advantage to access the nectar in long, tubular flowers.

**STAGE 1**

Bees are not very active during winter – but when the season starts to change, the hive is abuzz with activity. When flowers bloom, bees begin to forage for nectar to make more honey. The queen bee will mate in mid-air up to 24 times and then start laying eggs.

**STAGE 4**

Ten days later, the bees emerge from their cocoons as fully formed adults and begin to collect pollen and nectar with the other worker bees. Queen bees emerge a little earlier, at about six days of age.

At Walaja Broome Bush Honey, the team harvests honey made from the nectar of native plants. This is apprentice beekeeper Naomi Appleby.

Native bee is guni in the Gamilaraay language.

STAGE 2

After three days, the eggs hatch and larvae emerge. Each larva will be fed about 1300 times a day. They are fed by worker bees that have the special task of looking after the larvae, so these bees are called brood nurses. They feed the developing larvae food made from pollen and honey.

**DID YOU KNOW?**

**First Nations people use sugarbag honey as bush tucker and in bush medicine, as it has antibacterial and healing properties. The native bees that make it are stingless.**

STAGE 3

When the larvae are six days old, they are sealed in their own little chamber in the honeycomb. They then spin a cocoon around themselves and start to transform into a pupa.

# Cicadas

Australia is home to an astounding variety of cicadas, and all but a handful of our more than 230 species are found nowhere else on Earth. To many, they are simply percussionists, producing a soundtrack for warm summer evenings – but they lead fascinating lives, both below and high above the ground.

Cicada is galanj in the Dharug language.

**STAGE 1**

The cicada's song is made by the male – it keeps predators away and is also a mating call. The cicada is the loudest of all singing insects, and its song is sometimes loud enough to repel birds. Males 'sing' by vibrating a membrane on the sides of their bodies. Whether singing takes place during the day, at dusk, or both, depends on the species.

## Excellent timing

Greengrocer cicadas are recorded to spend around seven years underground as nymphs. One American genus, known as periodical cicadas, emerge from the ground in 13- or 17-year cycles. Some scientists suggest these cycles, which are indivisible prime numbers, help keep the cicadas safe from predators. Cicadas are preyed on by birds, bats, wasps and spiders.

During mass emergences of cicadas, various species of mammals, fish, amphibians, birds and reptiles will eat them. Because most predator populations run in shorter cycles – such as two, four or six years – these cicadas are less likely to emerge at the same time as their predators, which assists in their ongoing survival.

**STAGE 5**

The newly emerged cicada climbs up and clings to a tree. Here, it spends an hour or more, shedding its crunchy shell. It takes several more hours for its wings to become dry and sturdy enough for flight. Then it has a few weeks of flying freedom, in which to eat and mate, before dying.

## STAGE 2

As the male approaches the female, he switches to a quieter call. She makes a clicking sound with her wings if she likes his song, and mating commences. Females usually mate two or three times, laying eggs in the few days between matings.

## STAGE 3

The female cicada lays hundreds of eggs in grass stems, tree bark or on shrubs. The male and female both die, but the eggs hatch 6–7 weeks later, and the nymphs drop down and burrow into the ground, searching for a tree root to drink sap from.

**FACT**

**Cicadas are a bush food and are considered a good source of protein.**

## STAGE 4

The cicada nymphs spend at least nine months – and up to several years – underground, feeding on sap and moulting up to four times. When they reach full size and the conditions are right, the nymphs tunnel their way to the surface until they almost break through it. They settle in and wait for the right conditions, regularly emerging a day or two after rain.

Cicadas emerge from the ground, then from their hard shell.

# Quolls

Australia's four quoll species are easily recognised by their pointed snouts, long tails and spotted fur. Quolls have sharp teeth and strong jaws for tearing meat and crushing bones. Like the related Tasmanian devil, these fierce marsupials communicate loudly with hisses and screams. Quolls shelter in hollow logs or dens in forests, emerging mostly at night to hunt. The largest species, the spotted-tailed quoll, eats mammals such as possums, gliders and rabbits, as well as birds and reptiles. The smaller species eat mainly insects, frogs, fruit, small mammals, birds and lizards. Quolls are generally solitary outside of breeding season or when they visit communal latrines to mark their territory and socialise with each other.

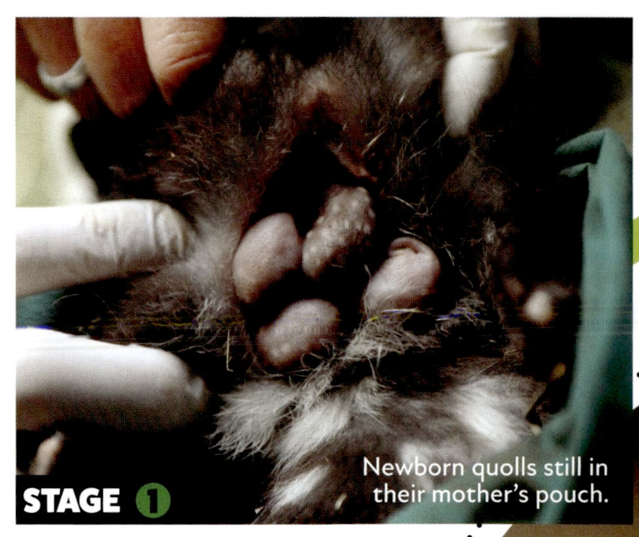

STAGE 1

Newborn quolls still in their mother's pouch.

After mating, a backwards-opening pouch develops on the female's belly. Three weeks later, she gives birth to up to 30 tiny, underdeveloped young. They make their way to her teats to feed, but as she only has six teats, those that don't latch on to one die. The baby quolls stay attached to the teat for 2–3 months as they grow and develop, feeding on their mother's nutritious milk.

## Quolls in danger

Once widely distributed across Australia and New Guinea, populations of quolls have shrunk due to habitat loss, disease and competition from introduced foxes and cats. These invasive species can cause havoc on the food web within an ecosystem. Sadly, feral cats in Australia are causing devastation to more than 400 native species – and have already contributed to the extinction of at least 20 mammals. The impact of feral cats and foxes, alongside other issues such as habitat destruction or cane toad poisoning, means quolls are dying faster than they can reproduce.

WESTERN QUOLL

## STAGE 2

After 2–3 months, depending on species, young quolls emerge from the pouch but stay close to their mum. She carries them on her back and feeds them in the den for six more weeks.

SPOTTED-TAILED QUOLL

## STAGE 3

When ready, young quolls leave their mother's territory to find and mark out their own, reaching full maturity after one year. Eastern quolls live an average of two years, while larger spotted-tailed quolls live four years.

The name quoll comes from the Guugu Yimithirr language.

EASTERN QUOLL

## True story

There's nothing less appetising than the thought of a toad sausage, a concoction of cane toad mince and a nausea-inducing chemical, but scientists hoped it would deter quolls and other animals from eating toxic cane toads, and they were right.

Cane toads are poisonous, so eating one can be fatal, but most animals don't know this. So, Dr Jonathan Webb and colleagues from the University of Technology Sydney fed captive northern quolls the cane toad sausages and confirmed they were then less likely to eat toxic cane toad bait. In contrast, wild quolls that hadn't been exposed to the toad-aversion sausages did take a chance on the bait – which meant that when cane toads arrived in their habitat, they would eat them and die.

Based on their results, the researchers were confident that wild quolls would develop an aversion to cane toads through introduction to the laced toad sausages. This will help prevent quoll extinctions.

Dr Georgia Ward-Fear, in a collaboration with Indigenous rangers in the Kimberley area of Western Australia, also successfully used chemical-laced cane toad sausages as an aversion measure with local wildlife, in preparation for the infestation of cane toads anticipated in the area.

# Wombats

These wonderful diggers are marsupials. This means that when a baby wombat is born, it is underdeveloped, so it is carried by its mother in a pouch on her stomach to continue growing. Wombats are found across Australia and can weigh up to 35 kg – about the same as an 11-year-old child. They live in burrows in the ground and come out at night to forage for grasses, bark and roots.

**FACT**

Wombats can grow to 100 cm long, reach speeds of up to 40 km/h in short bursts, and live for 15 years in the wild.

## Teamwork

There are three types of links in a food chain. Producers are plants – they produce nutrients through the process of photosynthesis. Consumers can't make their own food, so they feed on producers or other consumers to survive. Decomposers, such as fungi, feed on decaying organic matter and break it down, returning nutrients to the soil that the producers can use – and the cycle begins again.

PRODUCERS

CONSUMERS

The word wombat comes from the Dharug language.

DECOMPOSERS

## STAGE 1

When it is born, a baby wombat, called a joey, is very tiny – it is only about the size of a jellybean, with very thin skin and no hair. It can't see, but it has an excellent sense of smell, which it uses to find its way to its mother's pouch and to quickly crawl inside. Once in the pouch, the wombat joey attaches itself to its mother's teat, which swells so the baby stays attached. Here, it remains, drinking lots of fattening and nutritious milk, which helps it grow and also stops the joey from getting sick.

A backwards-facing pouch lets a wombat dig tunnels without getting dirt in it.

## STAGE 2

The joey will stay in its mother's pouch, drinking her milk, for up to 10 months. After about a month in the pouch, it will start to look more like a wombat, with strong legs and sharp digging claws. It continues to grow, and at about three months old, it will have developed thick hair and be able to open its eyes. At about five months old, it starts to explore the world, but it still stays close to its mother and will jump into the pouch if threatened.

## STAGE 3

When the joey is about a year old, it will start to use its big teeth to eat food, but it remains close to its mother. It will sometimes follow her out of the burrow to find food at night, but at other times, it will stay in the burrow by itself while she goes out to eat. The mother will rip up grass roots and drop them on the ground for her baby to eat. During this time, the joey starts putting on more weight as it gets used to its new diet and finding food. A joey will stay close to its mother for about two years before leaving her to build its own burrow.

### DID YOU KNOW?

**Wombat poo is cube-shaped as their intestines are an irregular shape, with two grooves that mould their scat into cubes.**

# Wedge-tailed eagles

The wedge-tailed eagle is the largest bird of prey in Australia. These birds can grow to have a wingspan (the measurement from the tip of one wing to the tip of the other when the wings are spread) of more than 2 m. They like to soar high in the sky, and they have very good eyesight, which helps them spot prey on the ground. They are called wedge-tailed eagles because when you look up at them from underneath, their tail feathers form a diamond, or a wedge, shape. Like all birds, wedge-tailed eagles begin their life in an egg.

### STAGE 1

Female and male wedge-tailed eagles pair up and work together to build a massive nest from sticks and twigs. The nest is built high off the ground in the fork of a tree or on a cliffside to avoid predators, and it can be up to 2 m wide. Every day, the male will put fresh leaves in the base of the nest. The female usually lays two eggs; after she lays the first one, she waits 2–4 days before laying the second. The eggs are pale grey, splotched with purple and brown and are round to oval in shape. They measure about 70 mm x 60 mm – approximately the same size as a goose's egg.

## Pecking order

Within an ecosystem, there are food webs – a matrix of food chains involving animals that either prey on or are preyed upon by other animals. For example, in the Kimberley region of Australia, the wedge-tailed eagle is one of the key predators in a food web incorporating organisms such as dingoes, wallabies, frogs, ants and spinifex.

Food webs work towards equilibrium. If the number of predators in an ecosystem increases, these predators consume more and more, decreasing populations of their prey. Due to dwindling prey numbers, it becomes harder for the predators to find food, which decreases their own populations. In this way, prey and predators achieve a relative equilibrium, although the food web can also be upset by the introduction of new or invasive species, extreme weather events, and human factors such as land-clearing or poison baiting.

### STAGE 4

After about four months, the chicks have grown all their juvenile feathers. They stay with their parents for a little bit longer, learning to hunt for themselves. When the chicks can look after themselves, they leave their parents and fly away to find their own territory. They are fully grown at about six years old and can live up to 20 years.

## STAGE 2

The male and female take it in turns sitting on the eggs to keep them at the right temperature. After about 40 days, the first egg will hatch, followed by the second egg a few days later. Baby eagles are called chicks and are covered in fluffy white down. They can't feed themselves to start with, so they must rely on their parents to place food directly into their mouths.

The male eagle does all the hunting at this stage, and the female uses her beak to shred the prey he brings back so she can feed the babies. Sometimes during extended periods of drought, wedge-tailed eagles will stop breeding, as there is not enough food available.

**DID YOU KNOW?**

**For people of the Kulin Nation in Victoria, the wedge-tailed eagle represents their Creator being Bunjil.**

Eagle is garriirl in the Gumbaynggirr language.

## STAGE 3

When the chicks are about two weeks old, they start to grow their first feathers. Both parents will now go hunting for food, leaving the chicks behind. When the chicks are about a month old, they no longer need to be fed by their mother. While they can't fly yet, they can now recognise food when it is brought to them and will eat the meat off the nest floor. They continue to grow in size and develop more feathers.

# Emus

These flightless birds live only in Australia. They can grow to 2 m tall, and have three strong toes with sharp toenail-like claws, which they use to protect themselves by kicking. They mostly eat plants, but will sometimes consume small insects such as grasshoppers and moths. They have two sets of eyelids, one for blinking and the other to keep dust out.

## Too hot!

As the climate continues to warm, the influence will be felt more heavily by certain species. In the ocean, coral reefs will bleach and warming waters will alter the distribution of many marine species. Australia is already a particularly hot, arid country, so rising temperatures are likely to impact on a number of our species.

Past heatwaves in Australia have seen widespread deaths in birds such as zebra finches and budgerigars. A large heatwave that struck southern central Australia in 1932 caused the death of many millions of birds, as the temperature reached at least 50 °C.

Emus prefer to live in a semi-arid habitat but breed in the cooler months. If temperatures continue to rise and more heatwaves occur, it may begin to alter the life cycle, distribution and population of this species.

**FACT**

Emus have very low, deep calls that sound a bit like a hollowed-out drum.

**STAGE 1**

Emus form breeding pairs during the summer months of December and January and remain together for about five months. They routinely patrol their territory, protecting it from intruders. The male emu builds a nest out of grass, bark and leaves in a sheltered hollow on the ground.

**STAGE 4**

After about three months, the camouflaged stripy down chicks are born with grows out, replaced with darker plumage. The male stays with the chicks for 6–18 months, defending them and teaching them how to find food.

## STAGE 2

Emus breed in the cooler months of May or June; the exact timing is determined by the climate because they nest during the cooler months of the year. Every second or third day during the mating season, the female lays one of an average of 11 (and as many as 20) very large, thick-shelled, dark-coloured eggs.

Emu is thinawan in the Gamilaraay language.

### DID YOU KNOW?

**From March to August, you can see the 'Emu in the Sky' from First Nations astronomy. It isn't formed by the stars but by the dark areas of the night sky.**

## STAGE 3

The male incubates the eggs. From this time on, he does not eat, drink, or go to the toilet, and he stands up only to turn the eggs, which he does about 10 times a day. Incubation takes 56 days, and the eggs hatch within a couple of days of one another. The chicks are about 12 cm tall when they are born.

# Green tree pythons

A green tree python moves through the forest almost silently. It uses the broad scales on its underside to grip branches and can stretch its body from branch to branch while only holding on with the end of its tail. It uses the end of its tongue to detect different smells and relies on that, along with its ability to sense body heat, to hunt at night.

## Home sweet home

Different animals require different shelters. Some, like hermit crabs, move from shell to shell. Others, such as termites, nesting birds and rodents, build their own shelter for protection from predators and to regulate their temperature and protect them from weather.

Green tree pythons live in the eastern rainforests of Cape York and are arboreal, meaning they live in trees. They coil around branches, looping a few coils of their body over a branch in a saddle position and then placing their head in the middle.

**STAGE 1**

Solitary creatures, green tree pythons use scent to attract potential mates. Females don't eat during gestation, which lasts 70–90 days. Then, they lay 5–32 eggs in a tree hollow and brood over the clutch for up to 50 days. They wrap their coils around the eggs to maintain the incubation temperature.

**FACT**

They are non-venomous but have long recurved teeth to grip their prey.

## STAGE 2

The eggs hatch at the start of the wet season. Baby green tree pythons are either bright yellow or red at birth and are about 30 cm long. Once hatched, the baby pythons are independent from their mother and one another. Juvenile pythons tend to stay in canopy gaps or along the edge of the forest.

### DID YOU KNOW?

**The Oenpelli python, or nawaran in the Kunwinjku language, is an important totemic animal to the Bininj people of western Arnhem Land.**

Green tree snake is giirring in the Gumbaynggirr language.

## STAGE 3

The pythons remain yellow or red for the first six months, turning green between 6-12 months. They will reach full maturity after 2–3 years, at which stage they will be an average length of 1.5 m. As they grow, they eat larger and larger prey, and the adults move further and higher into the rainforest.

# Crocodiles

Australia has two species of crocodile – the saltwater and the freshwater. The saltwater crocodile is the largest reptile in the world. The males can grow to be 6 m long and can live for 70 years. They are called saltwater crocodiles because they like to live in the ocean, but they can also live in freshwater rivers and billabongs. Freshwater crocodiles are smaller than the saltwater species and have longer snouts. They are only found in freshwater. Both types of crocodile start life as an egg in a nest by the water.

## Ideal conditions

Crocodile nests need to be at a specific temperature for the baby crocodiles to grow. The temperature also affects how many of the babies will be born male and how many will be born female. This is true for a number of reptilian species, including turtles, and also some bird species.

For saltwater crocodiles, the preferred temperature range is about 31 °C – 32 °C. Cooler temperatures produce females, and warmer temperatures produce males. If the temperature rises too high or falls too low, it might kill the baby crocodile, or cause it to be born with deformities.

**STAGE 1**

A pregnant female saltwater crocodile builds a very impressive nest that can take her up to two weeks to complete. It is called a mound and can be as long as 2.5 m. She picks her nest site very carefully to make sure it is above the high-tide mark but not so far away that it might dry out. The nest is made up of leaf litter or damp vegetation and mud.

**STAGE 4**

Once in the water, the hatchlings stay with each other in what is called a crèche and keep close to their mother. They remain in the shallows while they get used to their environment and grow. While the mother crocodile tries her best to keep them safe, many of her babies will be eaten by predators or other crocodiles. Once they are about eight months old, they start to move away from each other and find their own territories.

**STAGE 2**

The mother crocodile lays up to 70 eggs in her nest. She is very protective of her nest and will attack any predator that comes close. While the baby crocodile is still in the egg, it will begin to call out to its mother. This is known as yelping, and it signals to the mother that it is time for the baby to be born. Once the mother begins to hear her babies, she digs away at her nest until the eggs are exposed. The baby crocodiles then use a special tooth to crack open their shell. The mother helps her babies break through the shell by gently rolling the eggs around in her mouth.

**FACT**

Many crocodile eggs never hatch. Some are washed away in floods or dry out during drought, and some are eaten by predators.

**DID YOU KNOW**

**Some groups of First Nations people have the crocodile as their totem – it symbolises protection.**

Saltwater crocodile is dungalaba in the Larrakia language and is a totem of the Larrakia people of Darwin.

**STAGE 3**

Once the babies are out of their shells, the mother puts them in a special pouch in her mouth and takes them down to the water for their first swim. When they are born, the babies, called hatchlings, are about 25 cm long – smaller than a school ruler.

# Frogs

Of the world's 7500-plus frog species, more than 240 are native to Australia. Frogs are amphibians, spending part of their life in water and part of their life on land. They need to keep their skin moist, so they like to live in wet or damp places – often near ponds and lakes. All frogs start off as tiny eggs in or near water and then develop into tadpoles before becoming frogs.

## Weird but wonderful

**While most frogs follow a similar pattern to the life cycle outlined here, some frogs have unique systems for producing young.**

**The gastric-brooding frog became extinct in the 1980s, but Australian scientists recently managed to produce embryos out of cells from dead specimens. The gastric-brooding frog evolved one of the most incredible strategies for reproductive success ever – it swallowed its fertilised eggs and incubated the tadpoles in its stomach before giving birth to fully formed froglets via its mouth.**

**The female Surinam toad, on the other hand, allows the male toad to roll 60–100 fertilised eggs onto holes on her back. Skin grows over the holes, and the mother incubates the eggs there. When the time is right, the young punch out through the skin and emerge as toadlets!**

**SOUTHERN GASTRIC BROODING FROG**

Frog eggs in jelly, known as frogspawn.

**STAGE 1**

Frogs begin their life in an egg, which the female lays in water or a very wet place. She lays lots of eggs at once, and they are all covered in a mass of jelly-like material known as frogspawn.

The jelly-like coating provides support and protection for the growing frogs and also lets them breathe and absorb water.

Where the mother frog chooses to lay her eggs is very important. If there is not enough water covering the eggs, they can dry out. If there is too much water, the eggs could get swept away.

**STAGE 4**

Their front legs begin to grow and their long tails to shrink, and tadpoles finally begin to look like tiny frogs. Once their tails completely disappear, the tadpoles have transformed into froglets. A froglet stays in or near water and slowly learns how to be a grown-up frog – catching insects with its long, sticky tongue. Once it gets big enough, it moves away from where it hatched to find its own territory to live in.

Frog is gindjurra in the Gamilaraay language.

**STAGE 2**

Some eggs are eaten by fish and other pond animals, but some survive, and the babies keep growing. After a few weeks, the eggs hatch. It takes less time for the eggs to hatch in warm weather than it does in cold weather.

The tadpoles that emerge spend all of their time in the water. Some tadpoles look nothing like adult frogs, and in the beginning, they don't even have legs. They are oval-shaped and have a long tail they use as a rudder to move around. They also have feathery gills on the side of the head, which help them to breathe underwater. The tadpoles eat algae that grows in the water.

**FACT**

**Frogs don't need to drink water, as they absorb it through the skin.**

**GREEN TREE FROG**

**STAGE 3**

Tadpoles grow fast; when they are a few weeks old, they begin to change into frogs. First, they grow back legs. Then their gills start to disappear, and they begin to swim to the surface to breathe air for the first time.

# Seadragons

These incredible species are small fish that look very similar to seahorses. Australia has two seadragon species – the leafy seadragon and the weedy seadragon. Although they are about the same size, they both look very different. In seadragons, just like in seahorses, the male cares for the young.

## Born ready

Although baby seadragons are small when they're born, they are able to swim and see perfectly. While it takes them two years to reach their full size, they don't really need the father to look after them.

Some animals require more care when they are born. For instance, marsupials such as kangaroos give birth to very underdeveloped live young. The baby is pink, hairless and blind. It makes its way to the pouch following a track the mother has licked and it spends several months in the pouch, drinking milk and continuing to develop.

Some animals, such as frogs and butterflies, hatch from eggs into one form and undergo a process of transformation into their adult form. Other species are born fully developed but have to be taught how to hunt and survive, such as dingo puppies.

**STAGE 1**

During spring and summer, male and female leafy seadragons swim into shallow waters to find a mate. The female produces up to 250 brightly coloured eggs. While the female does this, the tail of the male gets bigger and grows little cups. The female then transfers the eggs to the male.

**LEAFY SEADRAGON**

**STAGE 4**

Baby leafy seadragons will eventually grow to be about 20 cm long and will be fully developed adults by the time they are two years old. They feed on small organisms such as plankton by sucking them into their snout.

Water dragon is magaam in the Gumbaynggirr language.

## STAGE 2

The male incubates the eggs for about a month, depending on how warm the water is. Sometimes, the eggs get coated in algae. Scientists think this helps hide the eggs from predators.

Weedy seadragon eggs.

**DID YOU KNOW?**

**The leafy seadragon can change colour to blend in with its environment.**

## STAGE 3

When the babies hatch, they look like miniature replicas of their parents, and they emerge wriggling and squirming from the egg, tail-first. They are not all born at once; it can sometimes take a week for all the eggs to hatch. The seadragons are about 2 cm long when they are born and can look after themselves straight away, although they are extremely vulnerable, and only a small number survive to adulthood.

STAGE 1

Male and female whales mate during the winter months while they're visiting warm tropical waters on their annual migration. Breeding takes place every 2–3 years, as a female humpback is pregnant (or gestates) for about 11 months. During the pregnancy, the mother will migrate to one of the poles during summer to eat krill, before returning to the Tropics to give birth. She gives birth to one calf, tail-first, which can weigh as much as a tonne.

# Humpbacks

Whales are massive, graceful marine mammals that journey across half the planet as they migrate between their breeding and feeding grounds. They mate and give birth in the warmer waters near the Equator, and then travel back towards the poles where their food supply (krill) lives in abundance during the summer.

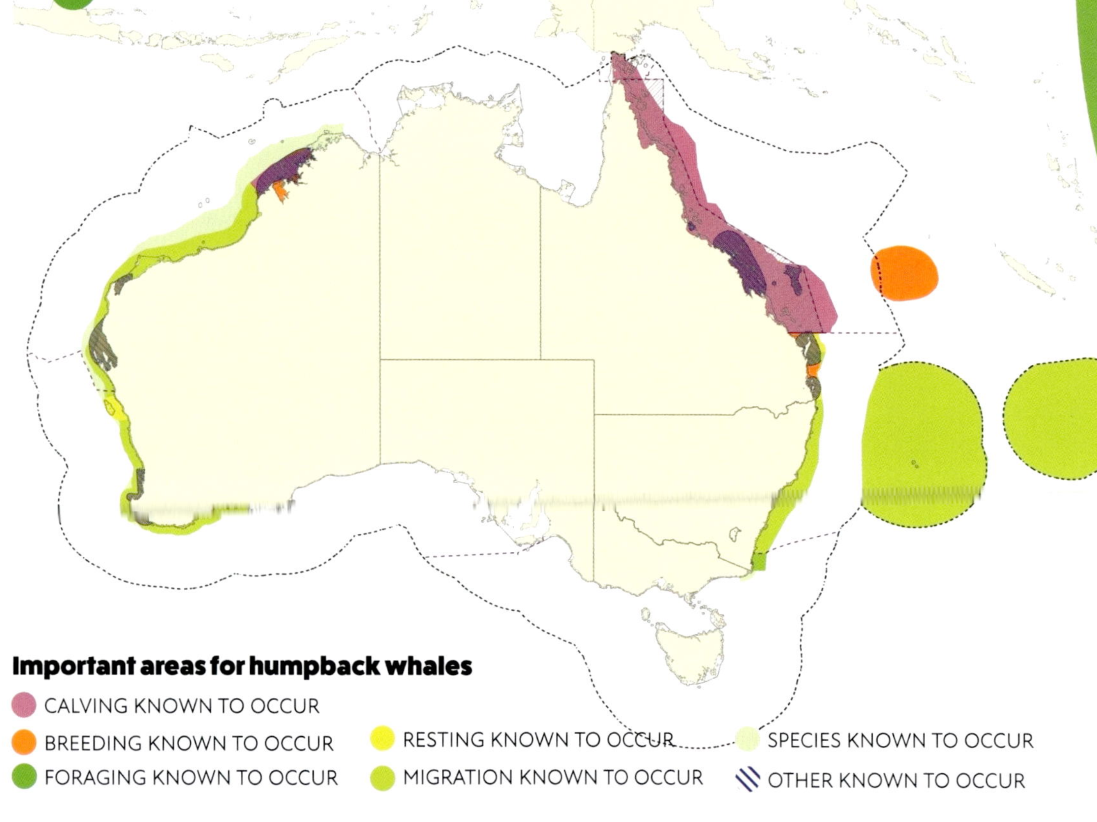

**Important areas for humpback whales**

- CALVING KNOWN TO OCCUR
- BREEDING KNOWN TO OCCUR
- FORAGING KNOWN TO OCCUR
- RESTING KNOWN TO OCCUR
- MIGRATION KNOWN TO OCCUR
- SPECIES KNOWN TO OCCUR
- OTHER KNOWN TO OCCUR

**STAGE 2**

The young whale will drink milk from its mother for 5–12 months and will grow to up to 9 m long. The mother whale will stay close to the baby until it is ready to live independently.

**DID YOU KNOW?**

**While all humpbacks use low-frequency sounds such as grumbles, snorts and thwops, only male humpbacks 'sing' as they attempt to attract potential mates.**

**STAGE 3**

Adolescent humpback whales leave their mother after about a year. Being social but solitary animals, they'll spend some time travelling alone, as well as with other humpbacks in pods. They eat up to 2500 kg of plankton, krill and small fish every day.

Humpback whale is mugga mugga in the Woppaburra language, and it is the totem of the Woppaburra people.

**STAGE 4**

By the age of about six, they are sexually mature adults that will start looking for a partner of their own.

# Creepy crawlies case study:
## Redfern Jarjum College

People encounter insects and other invertebrates every day. Unfortunately, these creepy crawlies are considered pests most of the time – but they are all part of Earth's biodiversity and play an important role in nature's processes.

At Redfern Jarjum College in Sydney, students collected some (mostly dead) bugs to have a closer look at them and discuss the similarities and differences.

They searched around the campus for some bugs, and one of the teachers brought some more from home. The students set up some microscopes and a magnifying glass in their library and called it a LAB-rary!

Each bug was carefully taped down to the glass and put under the microscope. In order to not squash what insect they were trying to look at, students were especially careful when adjusting the view up and down to focus the microscope.

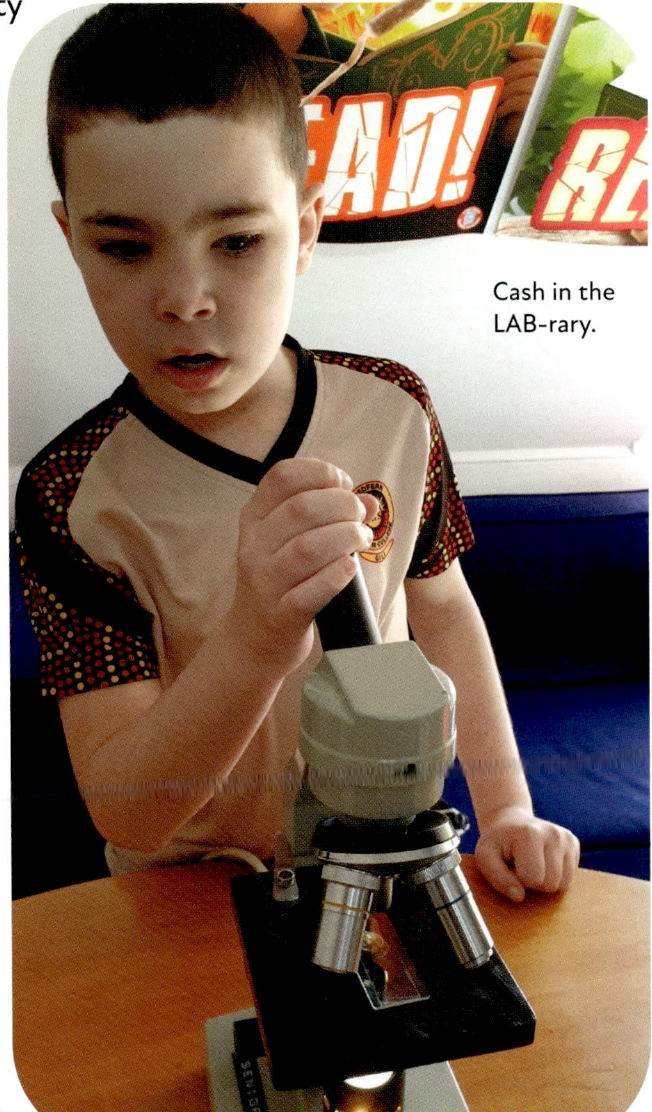

Cash in the LAB-rary.

**DID YOU KNOW?**

**Maggots seem to be very simple creatures with just a head and a body, but after a few days, they turn into flies.**

The beetle and pill-bug had hard shells. The flies and the beetle had six legs, but the pill-bug had seven pairs of legs plus two pairs of antennae. The students could see all the tiny hairs on the wings and body of the flies, as well as on the legs of the beetle.

The most bizarre creature was the maggot, which is actually a fly larva. This tiny caterpillar-like creature was pretty much just a head and a body, and through the microscope, the students could see right through the maggot's body.

The students agreed that looking at the bugs was a bit icky, but they still couldn't help going back for another look – or two!

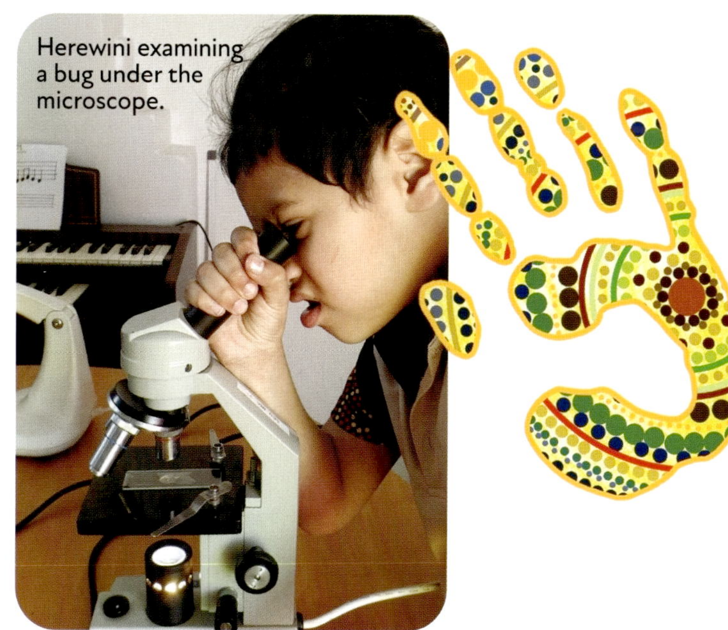
Herewini examining a bug under the microscope.

# Deadly Science

## Life cycles



Hardie Grant Children's Publishing
Wurundjeri Country
Level 11, 36 Wellington Street
Collingwood Victoria 3066
Melbourne | Sydney | San Francisco
hardiegrant.com/childrens
www.australiangeographic.com.au
ISBN: 9781761216633
First published 2022
This edition published 2025


**Series editor** Corey Tutt **Illustrator** Mim Cole / Mimmim
**Designer** Harmony Southern

**Publisher** Penelope White **Editor** Savannah Hollis with Olivia Brown
**Cover design** Andy Warren **Internal design** Hannah Janzen
**Production** Sally Davis

Printed in China by LEO Paper Products LTD

The paper this book is printed on is from FSC® certified forests and other controlled sources. FSC® promotes environmentally responsible, socially beneficial and economically viable management of the world's forests.

10 9 8 7 6 5 4 3 2 1

A catalogue record for this book is available from the National Library of Australia

## Picture credits

**Front Cover:** James Moffat/Australian Geographic (AG); Ego Guiotto/AG; Ray Sim/AG; Cameron Cope/AG; Kurit Afshen/Shutterstock (SS); Eric Isselee/SS; Artforwarm/SS; Radoslaw Maciejewski/SS. **2:** D. Bond/SS; Paul Looyen/SS; Ken Griffiths/SS. **3:** Kurit Afshen/SS; Aastels/SS; Rudmer Zwerver/SS; Johan Larson/SS; Point 01 Design/SS. **4:** Pstockfour/SS; Amy Lutz/SS; Larcsky789/SS. **5:** Kazakova Maryia/SS; Vladimir Mucibabic/SS. **6:** ausnative/SS; Netski/SS; KarenHBlack/SS; Bildagentur Zoonar GmbH/SS. **7:** Ken Griffiths/SS; Ken Griffiths/SS. **8:** LilKar/SS; Ihor Hvozdetskyi/SS; Daniel Prudek/SS; Maria T Hoffman/SS; Walaja Broome Bush Honey. **9:** Dredger/SS; bamgraphy/SS. **10:** aapi/SS; skynetphoto/SS; Simon Shim/SS; flyingv3/SS. **11:** Gerry Bishop/SS; Christina Rowe-CC BY-SA; Gerry Bishop/SS. **12:** Aussie Ark; Craig Dingle/SS; Eric Isselee/SS. **13:** Aussie Ark; Kevin Stead/AG; Esther Beaton/AG. **14:** R.J. Low/SS; zabavina/SS. **15:** Mitch Reardon/AG; Jonas Boernicke/SS; S. Aratrak/SS. **16:** Nico Faramaz/SS; Ecopix/SS; Chris Watson/SS; Mickey Eric Mackwan/SS. **17:** Auscape/UIG/SS; Tim Webster/AG. **18:** Robert N Tonn/SS; colacat/SS; K.A.Willis/SS; doodlart/SS. **19:** John Carnemolla/SS; Martchan/SS. **20:** Ego Guiotto/AG; Morris Mann/SS; Eric Isselee/SS. **21:** Paul Tessier/SS; David Hancock/AG; Kurit Afshen/SS. **22:** Photoongraphy/SS; Ger Metselaar/SS; Alizada Studios/SS; Sylvie Lebchek/SS. **23:** rookiephoto19/SS; Ego Guiotto/AG. **24:** YueStock/SS; Andrew Lam/SS; Dr Morley Read/SS; Kevin Stead/AG. **25:** Savo Ilic/SS; Ken Griffiths/SS; W. de Vries/SS. **26:** Marben/SS; Dirk van der Heide/SS; Rudie Kuiter/OceanwideImages.com; Anan Kaewkhammul/SS. **27:** Katherine OBrien/Canva; Karen Gowlett-Jones. **28:** Alberto Loyo/SS; William Drumm/SS; © Commonwealth of Australia 2013. **29:** Imagine Earth Photography/SS; Justin Berken/S–S; Konrad Mostert/SS. **30:** Bob Pool/SS; Redfern Jarjum College (RJC); RJC. **31:** RJC; RJC; RJC; RJC; irin-k/SS.